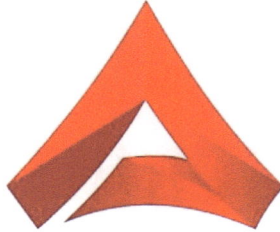

APARTMENT
PRESCRIPTION

*How we took the prescription for freedom and time and
turned it into a hands-off landlord passive investment.*

GEORGE S. WU, MD

RHEA VICTORIA B. RAZON-WU, MD

APARTMENT PRESCRIPTION 2.0

Rhea Victoria B. Razon-Wu, MD

George S. Wu, MD

Apartment Prescription 2.0

Rhea Victoria B. Razon-Wu, MD

George S. Wu, MD

A1 Dragon Enterprise, LLC

Library of Congress Cataloging-in-Publication Data

Razon-Wu MD, Rhea

Wu, MD George S.

ISBN: 979-8-9860868-6-6

Printed in the United States of America.

Dedicated to

My wife, Rhea Victoria B. Razon-Wu, MD

My 2 kids, George Razon-Wu, Jr and Jaden Razon-Wu

My parents, Joyce Wu and Ching Chung Wu

My parents-in-law, Haydee Blanco Razon and Hospicio Sales Razon

My sister, Ines and her family, Victor, Isabella

My brother-in-law, Lyle and his family, Maria, Mariano, Adriella

My grandmother, Wu Lin BaoKway

My grandmother-in-law, Mayor Victoria Yap Blanco

All our relatives in Taiwan, Philippines and USA that are too many to mention

(Please know that you are all remembered, and we are forever grateful).

CONTENTS

CHAPTER 1

INTRODUCTION

This little guide is a supplement to the real estate book Apartment Prescriptions authored by my wife. I am someone who loves the art of pure medicine. When I was in high school, I was determined to become a doctor. As a first-generation Chinese immigrant from Taiwan, I grew up poor, dirt poor – the first town we lived in NJ was a stone's throw away from the dangerous car-jacking metropolis of Newark NJ. The first apartment we lived in had cockroaches – very tiny ones without wings—that would scurry into hiding whenever we turned on the kitchen lights to enter. In fact, my sister and I had a game to see who could stomp the most with our sneakers.

I graduated first in my high school, scored a nearly perfect SAT score, won a full 4-year tuition-and-board scholarship to Northwestern University, graduated college in 3 years, went to medical school, and eventually became a radiologist. (My sister eventually became a Harvard-trained dermatologist.)

I love being a radiologist. I love interpreting the difficult image cases; many radiologists "cherry pick" the normal cases but I am the opposite – I run and embrace the leftover challenging cases. I'm honored when the pediatric surgeon comes down and says, "George, I don't know what to do with this kid. He's been to the emergency room 3 times, he's had imaging at outside hospitals, we've treated him, and he's getting worse. What do you think?" All my life I've identified with being the archetype of a troubleshooter – the person that solves the most difficult cases, in and out of a medicine. I don't enjoy reading the normal cases; the routines don't tingle my spine. I love the intermingling of pain and the joy of interpreting challenging imaging cases – in 2021 I was one of two national winners of the *Radiology* Diagnosis Please competition for solving the most unknown radiology cases.

I tell you this information to show you that I love medicine in its purest form but hate all the accompanying politics, interference from government and insurance, the rise of corporate medicine, the slow degradation of physician autonomy, the declining reimbursement, the bureaucratic rules and so on. Physicians today feel overworked and unappreciated. I also share the above to show that I leverage my God-given analytical skills in radiology and use it in my real estate investing. The contents of the box (radiology vs real estate investing) may change but my analytical approach and my drive to master the material are unchanged.

Early in my career, I saw how all the taxes took away half of my paycheck. Then I was diagnosed with trigger finger in my right thumb from all the clicking on the mouse – I would hear an audible clunk in the interphalangeal joint on flexion. I splinted my hand, and it got better, but there is a nagging fear that I'm one catastrophe away. I upped my disability insurance, but I wanted to play offense and not just defense in terms of my finances.

I realized that despite my love of medicine I needed a backup plan to wisely invest the money I had made. I gained essentially no financial education from my parents, college, or medical school. So, I did what I've done all my life: I put on my troubleshooting analytical hat and started to experiment.

First, I tried stock investing of all forms – day trading, shorting penny stocks, following Motley Fool, and so forth. After losing $25 k, I cut my losses; investing in stocks just didn't make my heart sing. Then I investigated online commerce – I was even ready to go to China and visit a manufacturing factory to make products for me to sell here but then decided against it. Then I was looking into selling mugs on Etsy. I was chasing after every ad that flashed in my Facebook profile or read in a book.

All this time, my wife had ventured into real estate. However, it took me many years to fully buy into real estate. Real estate is **not** a get rich quick scheme; it is more a get rich slow scheme. It was the slow –but steady—part that didn't initially excite. In stock investing, it's potentially possible to double your money in less than a year; passively investing into a multifamily apartment usually requires a 5-year hold period to double one's money. However, real estate investing offers a peace of mind that is difficult to find in other investments. When I wasn't doing radiology, I was studying real estate, attending conference, networking, etc. I know many of my colleagues are successful investing in stocks-- continue to do that! However, it doesn't hurt to diversify into real tangible assets like real estate.

CHAPTER 2

VERSION 1.0 of the Real Estate Journey

My wife and I have experience with both the active and passive side of real estate investing.

On the active side, we have bought 67 units (single family to small six units) with our money along with the typical bank financing. I work full-time as a diagnostic radiologist, and my family medicine trained wife, is a stay-at-home mother and a real estate professional. We, or mainly my wife, manages the properties – from finding new deals, underwriting the deals, doing the property inspection, overseeing the renovations, finding tenants, managing tenants, collecting rents, etc. The beauty of active investing is the sense of control. There is nothing like the feeling of walking through your rental properties, looking at the beautiful new siding that you orchestrated for the property or the contemporary design of the landscaping that you brought to life from your imagination into reality. There is a direct one-to-one correlation between what we envision and what we bring to reality in the world. It's almost analogous to the story in Genesis in the Bible where God called forth creation by saying "Let there be light" and then there was light. Being an active manager allows a feeling of being an active creator or an artist—what you envision, or think is good can come into fruition in a brief time span.

However, with the good, also comes the challenging aspect. For example, below are a few real examples:

1. The tenant calling us on Thanksgiving late in the evening with no hot water. We still remember entering the cold basement and seeing the broken and flooded hot water tank. The stress of calling multiple plumbers and finding out that the advertisement of 24/7 service doesn't really apply to holidays, especially late at night.

2. The tenant calling us at 2 am because of the "smell of gas" in the house. Trudging to the property at that time, we see the street walled off by a sea of police cars and fire trucks and a flurry of emergency personnel entered the property. The gas company employee showed up and determined that it was not a natural gas leak. The smell it turned out was from a skunk that had deployed its pungent odor next to the property.

3. The ticking time bombs that lurk that you don't know about. One of our properties had an unused oil tank that sat in the basement, a remnant of the olden days when oil was pumped into an oil tank that was then used to heat a house. We didn't think too much of the oil tank until one day on a maintenance visit, we noticed corrosion on the underside of the tank. The plumber came on site and promptly removed the tank. He told us it was a good thing we noticed this issue earlier as an oil leak would have been an environmental hazard costing thousands to clean up.

4. Being a landlord requires one to be a troubleshooter in

many respects. Suppose the tenant calls you and says that the brand-new drier always stops 15 minutes in the drying process. At this point, you have several options. You can call appliance repair, but they will charge $125 dollars just to visit and diagnose the problem. That doesn't include the cost of the repair. The drier itself may cost $500 dollars. For convenience you may pay for the repair, but that will wipe out your cash flow for the month. So, in our situations, as landlords, we will troubleshoot the situation first. That usually involves me first reading the manual online, googling up potential solutions, and going to the property in person. In this situation, it turned out the contractor, who had been doing renovations on the property in the dead of winter, had stuffed a rag into the drier vent outlet duct so that the frigid air would not enter into the property. He forgot to remove the rag later when the renovation was done. So, when the new drier was connected to the drier vent, it was trying to push exhaust air through the blocked vent, causing the machine to overheat. I felt proud for solving this issue. However, the cost was loss of my time.

Financially, we don't want to downplay the benefits that being an active landlord provides. My wife qualifies as a real estate professional which is an IRS designation where "the taxpayer meets both of the following requirements: (1) more than half of the personal services performed in all trades or businesses during the tax year were performed in real property trades or businesses in which the taxpayer materially participated; and (2) the taxpayer performed more than 750 hours of services during the tax year in real property trades or businesses in which he or she materially participated (Sec. 469(c)(7)(B))."

Basically, it means my wife does a lot of active real estate. The beauty of a real estate professional is that she can take the passive losses of being a landlord and apply the losses to my active W2 income as a radiologist. So, if I make $400k as a radiologist, if my wife is not a real estate professional, I would take home about $200k after subtracting for all the taxes such as federal, state, etc. However, because my wife is a real estate professional, I get to take home all $400k.

When I first heard about this from my wife, I said that is unfair. Physicians work so hard for all these years. I can personally remember taking overnight call as a radiology resident, and one night being so tired, that I fell asleep and banged my head on the computer monitor in front of me. Add to it the stress of being perfect in my radiological reads so I don't hurt my patients or get sued. Many times, I come home from work tired, with my kids wanting to play catch or read a book, and yet not really being 100% present with them, knowing that I had more medical stuff to do after work, such as ruminating about the difficult case I saw earlier or the new journal articles that I had to read.

I asked my wife why the government allows these kinds of deductions for those in real estate. It turns out that the government incentivizes people that are providing housing for the community. These deductions are what motivates people to become landlords and provide a service to the community. These special deductions exist in other industries such as farming. It's exceedingly rare for a farmer to pay taxes – the government wants to incentivize farmers to continue to grow food otherwise we would all go hungry.

In summary, for the right individual, being an active property owner can be a lot of fun, with great financial benefits. One of the other financial benefits, is that if you own multiple properties, you will grow your net worth. However, it's not for everyone, especially if you are a full-time physician. This method works best if one-half of the couple works as a physician to generate the ordinary income while the other spouse takes on the role as the real estate professional to generate the deductions. However, just a warning: the spouse must LOVE being an active property owner. He/she should walk into the situation with eyes wide open, fully aware of the benefits and challenges. Being a full-time property owner is like being a full-time mother to a bunch of children, some of whom are recalcitrant. You must be the type of parent that enjoys the process of parenting multiple children. Tenants sometimes are like little hens that need to be herded – sometimes rewarding and many times stress inducing. As a landlord, one must enjoy being hands-on, physically, and mentally.

CHAPTER 3

VERSION 2.0 of the Real Estate Journey

One of the questions that we often get from family and friends is how to do real estate. For many years we would tell them about how to do active real estate investing, but many of them failed or just did not enjoy it.

One good friend was a fellow radiologist who likened his work as radiologist to that of a Whack-A-Mole, a carnival game where one takes a soft hammer and pounds furry moles that randomly pop up from holes on the table. The player uses quick reflexes to hammer down as many of these moles as possible. Initially exhilarating, the work became monotonous. The never-ending portable chest x-rays, the emergency room head CTs, and the phone calls from techs and referring clinicians were tasks that were to be accomplished as fast as possible. Radiology was one big Whack-A-Mole endeavor, one that was futile and non-fulfilling. The blur of studies felt like weeds in the ground – you pull one weed up and another would replace it. Doing this year after year really deadened his senses and enjoyment of the field. I think most doctors, no matter what specialty, have similar sentiments of being on a treadmill of clinical work that is increasing by the passing year.

He really wanted to replicate what my wife and I were doing in real estate, but his wife just really had no interest in real estate. He would buy properties and have a second job as landlord, besides being a full-time radiologist.

After seeing this iteration several times with other friends, we were stumped. Starting out as a property owner initially is a lot of work and "bruising" to one's ego, finances, and time. I liken it to when I started rollerblading. I would fall so many times in the parking lot in the park. The blows were cushioned by the protective armor of thick knee pads, wrist guards, and a helmet but it was embarrassing having passer-by joggers and walkers secretly laughing at my spectacle of trying to balance. Eventually, though with practice, you start gliding and flying by the same joggers. Being a landlord is the same process. In the beginning, it's trial and error even with good guidance. One can read all about rollerblading, but one will never learn to rollerblade until you do it and fall.

So, we started brainstorming if there was a way to "bring" family and friends into the properties we were buying and make money both for ourselves and for them. We envisioned being the expert pilots of flying the real estate plane and bringing family and friends along for the ride.

After much exploration, we stumbled upon real estate syndication. This syndication term is unfamiliar to most people – common associations would be like a mafia syndication as in the Godfather movie. It's actually a fancy term that means the pooling of capital or resources to tackle bigger projects. Those big apartment buildings with 200 units or the new developments you see around town were likely financed by people pooling their money together so that they could buy a much nicer property than what they could buy by themselves individually. In fact, in 1961, 3300 investors came together and contributed $10k each to acquire the Empire State Building in NY. A NY times article describes this deal as a "treasure investment and an echo of an era when New York's rising middle class nervously put all their meager savings into a tower that touched the sky." Source: NYT There is something very romantic and poetic picturing these investors putting their faith into something bigger than themselves.

The people that are the "pilots" of the syndication are known as the sponsors or the general partners (GP). Usually it's a small group (<5) who are experts in multifamily real estate (it doesn't have to be multifamily, but this is the asset type we are familiar with; people will syndicate other assets such as self-storage units, mobile homes etc.) I like to think of the GPs as the US Army's Special Forces Teams. Each soldier, besides the base proficiency in the art of being a warrior, also has an additional focus, such as weaponry, communications, medical, and engineering.

Similarly, the GPs all have a basic knowledge of all the facets of real estate. However, each member usually has an additional specialty. One person may be the extrovert, a networker of people. Another usually lives in the target market and has intimate knowledge of the apartments there. Another is the underwriter who crunches the financial numbers and creates the projection models. Another is the "net worth" person – to secure a loan for the apartment, the net worth of the group needs to be above the loan amount. Another member may be brought on because of the experience of having led many other past deals. However, each team member needs to know everything well. Just like in the Special Forces, each member is cross trained into different disciplines but also has a special niche of skills.

The sponsorship team will have a history of many past successful syndications. Usually, if the team does not have this past track record of many successful syndication, it is unlikely the selling broker will award the deal to the team as the broker is worried that the deal may not close. Furthermore, a weak team will have trouble securing a mortgage as mortgage brokers are loathe to loan out millions of dollars to a team that has not shown a successful track record of being able to carry out a business plan on such a large scale.

The GP team will look at hundreds of deals to find the few that meet criteria. Generally, GPs are looking for large multifamily apartments (say greater than 100 units) in a very hot location. When I say hot, I mean a city where the population growth is explosive, where thousands of people are moving in, where the economic base is diverse, where the laws are landlord friendly (landlord unfriendly would be states where evictions of rotten tenants would take long months and large legal fees), and where the purchase price of a single family is too expensive such that people are displaced into renting. For example, the median home price in South Tampa is $575,000; most people cannot afford the mortgage for such prices and are forced to rent.

The GPs will "stress test" the property by making sure that there is a healthy breakeven occupancy such that the property can still manage its debt. A hypothetical stress test via financial modeling is done to see what the lowest percent occupancy is (i.e., worst case financial scenario) that would allow the apartment to still be cash flowing; the good properties are the ones that allow 60-75 % occupancy and is still cash flowing. So, the GPs know exactly at what level of occupancy the apartment is not able to meet the debt requirements i.e., pay the mortgage. The GPs are the ones that sign off on the mortgage loan – the passive investor has no liability beyond the money put in.

There are different strategies in multifamily apartment investing. The ones we like best as GPs is "stabilized multifamily with value add." "Stabilized" means its 90 % occupied for at least 90 days; we don't want apartments in distress where only 60% of the units are rented and the property is losing money. The "value add" component is to purchase apartments in places like Tampa or Dallas or Phoenix where the rents are growing organically without renovations or rehab; on top of that we do a light-to-moderate "value add" to force appreciation in the price of the property. We execute the business plan of doing renovations usually in a period of 2 years (maximum 3 years) while being careful to keep the occupancy level stable. The plan is then to sell the property in five years.

One thing that is not apparent to most people is that in

multifamily investing we can borrow from the bank 80 to 85 % of the sale price of the apartment with a long-term mortgage at say 3 %. At the time of this writing in the end of 2021, US inflation hit a 39-year high of 6.8%, as reported in the Wall Street Journal. So, if we bought the property and left it untouched (no value-add renovations) that debt, because it's at 3 % versus the 6.8 % inflation, is **not** a liability. Instead, the debt is an asset — the inflation "eats" away at the debt and allows us investors to get free equity.

The rent leases because they are yearly renewal can be increased with inflation if the property is in a hot market; the additional renovations will allow further increases in rent above inflation. The expenses such as utilities and insurance for the property also go up in price but go up at a slower rate than inflation. (Economic experts are saying that inflation will continue to rise to as high as 15% because of all the free money that is being printed, and the fact that the dollar is no longer tied to gold.) The above may be technical but the point is that with the rising inflation, investing in real estate, which has always been attractive even in a dour economy, is even more alluring as an inflation hedge.

So, let us get to the nitty-gritty of money. The target is to give on average 7-8% preferred return to the passive investor every year, typically in a monthly or quarterly distribution. Suppose you invest $100 k into the deal. So, each year on average you would get $8,000 dollars if 8% annual average return; this money would come from the rental income from the property. Usually in the first year, because GPs are doing renovations with some units empty, you may get say $3000, which means you are short $5000 ($8k -3k). That $5000 will be given to you in the following year say year 2, where $8k+$5k or $13k, would be returned to you. Furthermore, this return is preferred. In other words, the GP team doesn't get paid until every passive investor is paid out the $8k, and then the GP catches up after that, usually in an 80/20 or 75/25 split i.e., 80% to the passive investors and 20 % to the sponsorship team. This preferred return structure shows confidence of the sponsorship team in the deal as the GPs don't partake in the profit share until the passive investors hit their hurdle of 8% annual return.

So, at this point from years 1 through 5, you've made $8000 multiplied by 5 years or $40k from the cash flow distribution from the rental income of the property. The beauty of this distribution is that it is untaxed, unlike dividends from the stocks. Then on year 5, the property will be sold; at that point, you will receive the original $100 k you put in plus a portion of the profit on the sale, say $60k. So, at the end of five years, you will get back the original capital invested of $100k, the $40k profit split from the rents during years 1-5, and the $60k profit split from the sale of the apartment – the total is $200 k, which is 2x of your original investment.

I want to go back and explain why the $40 k from the profit split from the rents is untaxed. The reason is that the apartment will show huge losses on paper. The explanation is technical. A typical real estate asset is depreciated 27.5 years; with larger assets like multifamily, a specialized CPA is hired called a cost segregation expert to find objects in the property that are eligible for faster or accelerated depreciation. Usually about a third of the asset can be depreciated in year 1 of ownership of the property.

Let's do a back-of-the envelop example. Suppose you own a $10 million apartment. Instead of the asset being depreciated $10 million/ 27.5 years or $363k a year, $10 million/3 or roughly $3 million of the apartment can be depreciated in year one thanks to the magic of cost segregation. Furthermore, suppose that the apartment has $7 million dollars in mortgage and $3 million dollars in equity (i.e., the amount of money everyone puts into the deal). If as a passive investor, you put in $300 k investment in the deal, you would be a 10% owner ($300k/$3 mil) of the asset. As a result, you would be privy to 10% of the $3 mil depreciation or $300k depreciation losses. The IRS considers this depreciation loss to be a passive loss so you can't deduct this against your W2 income, which is active income. Passive loss usually deducts passive income. ("Passive income includes regular earnings from a source other than an employer or contractor. The Internal Revenue Service (IRS) says passive income can come from two sources: rental property or a business in which one does not actively participate, such as being paid book royalties or stock dividends." Source: www.bankrate.com)

However, that depreciation value is going to be much larger than the annual cash flow from the project. So, suppose you got

$8k in cash flow that year but the depreciation was supposed to be $15k. In that case you won't pay taxes on the distribution. However, when the property is sold in year 5, you will have to "recapture" the depreciation i.e claim the depreciation as income and pay taxes on it. You might be wondering if we really gained anything? In fact, there are 2 main benefits. First, the tax rate on the recapture of the depreciation is less than ordinary income tax. Second, you got to pay taxes 5 years later when the value of the money is less. (As an aside, some people tell me that they hold REITS (real investment trusts) and don't need to invest in actual real estate. The downside to REITS is that because you don't hold a real asset you don't get the benefits of real estate depreciation and your dividends are taxed as ordinary income (physicians have an ordinary tax rate of 35% or higher) whereas the dividend from passive investing is usually tax-free. As a passive investor, you get the tax benefits as you own a piece of property, just with a smaller share.)

So, these passive losses are carried year after year until year 5 where the losses become active and potentially can deduct active income. Caveat: the tax laws are constantly changing, and I'm not a CPA so please check with the details of your CPA as to how best utilize this deduction in terms of your own unique tax situation.

Why does the IRS allow such a favorable tax profile for real estate? The IRS wants investors to come into neighborhoods and rehab the apartments for workforce housing and improve the neighborhoods. When investors do what the government and IRS wants us to do, the IRS rewards investors like us with tax breaks for improving the living environment of the population. GPs are not going into glitzy areas like Manhattan and buying an A+ property and doing nothing; usually they are going into a gentrifying community, investing money, and improving the apartments/communities.

So great, suppose you are interested in this passive real estate investing and want to participate as a passive investor. Some people will go to real estate crowdfunding sites that help facilitate real estate transactions (both good and bad deals). On these sites, one will see many real estate deals all with similar numbers. The problem is that the sponsors will be unknown to you.

I have read books that recommend attending local meetups to meet the GPs that sponsor these deals; this option is possible, but it involves talking to a lot of people to meet a few GPs. For example, at some of these meetups, I often meet contacts who try to sell me their services, such as roofers, repair people, etc.

To save time, what my wife and I personally did was to pay a lot of money to join a club of GPs. These clubs will hold weeklong meetings in an exotic location a few times a year for everyone to get to know one another. Usually, there will be informational lectures during the day of how to be a better GP and nighttime networking events. Spending a week with the same group of people allows us to really get a feel of the energy of the person. We also learn the inside details of the deals that have gone well and those that haven't. It is during these meeting that GP teams will form.

From there, we invested passively into other GP deals as limited partners. We invest passively in other GP deals to diversify our real estate portfolio. The properties that we actively manage are located in one town in central PA. There is a risk being concentrated in only one location. Through real estate syndication, we are able to invest outside of our primary location into other markets such as Dallas, Texas.

We also became involved on the active side of real estate syndications by becoming GPs. The GP team is the most vital component of real estate syndication. A good GP team can salvage a bad real estate deal while a subpar GP team can sink even an excellent real estate deal.

The process of a passive investor finding and vetting a good GP team is like finding a surgeon. Suppose you needed an elective cholecystectomy. You might ask a friend or family member if they ever had the procedure done. I know at work other radiologists will send a group email asking for recommendations for a good surgeon. But the best way would be to ask fellow surgeons or surgical residents or anesthesiologists – the people actually in the OR room. Of course, this takes extra work if you don't have that inside connection. So, to find a great surgeon or GP team is not so straightforward.

Ultimately, the decision boils down to trust and basic understanding of this investment model. As a passive investor, you are leveraging the GP team to hunt for a great deal in a great submarket, underwrite and financially model the finances, mitigate risk, sign on the loan, and manage the property. Some of the barriers to entry are the minimum investment requirements which on average is around $75 to $100k. The goal is to double your money in 5 years (very attainable target) but remember that the money put in is illiquid; if you suddenly need money for an upcoming event, it's very hard to get your money out, unlike a stock investment where you can click a button and sell. (Some GPs will offer a preferred return of say 10-12 % interest per year for 2 years. In this way, one gets higher return, earlier return of capital, but no participation in the upside of the final profit from selling the property.)

As a passive investor, you come along for the ride – you don't have direct control in the business plan. For example, you don't decide how much each unit should be rented for or what parts of the apartment should be renovated. On the other side, this lack of control in the business plan execution is an expected positive feature of passive investing; if one didn't want to delegate these decisions to the GP team, then one should go the active route as discussed above.

The risk is of course that you could lose money. The GPs mitigate the risk by buying apartments that are stabilized value add (93% occupancy or so) and not developments in distress. These apartments already have tenants living in it and paying rent. Because the property makes rental income, it will deliver distributions to investors on a monthly or quarterly basis; some people mistakenly believe they receive no cash from years 1-5 and then get back all the returns in year 5. Remember this property will be paying you cash all throughout years 1 through 5. And when the property is being improved the value of the property goes up so when the property is sold in year 5, everyone shares in the final profit from the sell. Unlike stocks, because the apartment is a tangible asset that you can touch and feel, it's nearly impossible for the property to lose 30-40% of its value overnight, as can happen in stock investments.

Another benefit of large multifamily apartments is if a few tenants leave, there is no financial concern because of the economies of scale. Whereas in active real estate, especially in the beginning, if one of your units goes vacant, it can be stressful financially as there is no economies of scale to absorb the loss. Along the same lines, with an investment of $100k, one cannot buy a 100-unit apartment complex. However, if you have fifty investors putting in $100 k each, then it is possible to buy a 100-unit apartment complex with professional property management.

CHAPTER 4

CONCLUSION

Lastly, for some people, money and finances is a taboo topic. I think of money as a vehicle to help humanity. Without financial wealth and freedom, people cannot help society beyond their immediate friends and family. For most people, becoming financially free is a way to no longer be a slave to the demands of outside circumstances – instead one can live life on one's own terms. I once heard someone tell me "Money won't make you happy, but how you use it can."

Most people don't know how to buy a large apartment complexes. For these people, if they are interested in real estate investing (most people should be as they are too pigeonholed into stocks and mutual funds from their 401ks), they can invest alongside experienced people like us, which allows us to scale and buy bigger and better apartments while at the same opening the doors for busy, non-real estate people to passively participate in the returns that are generated without having to be the real estate experts.

Let's Go! Wealth Can't Wait!

Let's Go! Wealth Can't Wait!

Facebook.com/ApartmentPrescription/

https://www.linkedin.com/in/apartmentprescription

Youtube.com/channel/UCGdp0PGO1NjVOitZ96tnYZw

APARTMENT
PRESCRIPTION

Learn more at

www.apartmentprescription.com

www.apartmentprescription.com

www.ingramcontent.com/pod-product-compliance
Lightning Source LLC
Chambersburg PA
CBHW041718200326
41520CB00001B/158